T0294016

How Wild?

How Wild?

POEMS: 1987–1989

LINDA CRANE

BARRYTOWN/STATION HILL

Published by Barrytown/Station Hill Press, Inc., Barrytown,
NY, 12507, as a project of the Institute for Publishing Arts, Inc.,
in Barrytown, New York, a not-for-profit, tax-exempt organiza-
tion [501(c)(3)], supported by grants from the New York State
Council on the Arts.

Cover painting by Thorpe Feidt
Detail from *July Triptych: The Ambiguities 418-420*
acrylic on canvas, 12 IN. X 34 IN. (whole), 2005

Author photo on p.47 by Ann Fuller

typeslowly designed
Printed by McNaughton & Gunn, Inc.

Library of Congress Cataloging-in-Publication Data available.

Crane, Linda, 1945-2000.
  How wild? : poems, 1987-1989 / Linda Crane.
    p. cm.
  ISBN 1-58177-105-3
  I. Title.

PS3603.R384H69 2006
811'.6--dc22
                                        2006002157

Contents

The Night Sky

(Solely to Know) — *for Thorpe Feidt*

To the night sky I lay bare myself,
disclose my body to the stars.

I am aware how they touch me,
point for point enter my eyes, pores and being.

They embrace me til I lavish in wholeness,
            dense with stars,
and love is exquisite beyond perception.

Under the night sky — does it begin or end?   could
it ever cease before becoming me?

or before Linda becomes starlight? — white sea birds,
cats of antiquity, beckoning kelp,

and the gracious whiteness of lilt-petaled shad, rooted
in the star-field, encourage me.

From them I can no longer bear
the separation.

With nothing to lose I step out
and cross the gulf of what is not real,

open my glad eyes that can behold
there is nothing to fear

and breathe the stars into awareness
of myself and the ecstasy
of creation.

10/87

Reciprocity

it already happens
it already is
Already I'm grateful
Already I'm giving something to you
Already everything is mine and yours
   Even before we speak of this
we mean the world
   to each other

being is enough.
there is no living
    to make.

together

out of no where
comes the taste of almonds and fruit.
He is calling me across
   my dreams.

How simple to go by the milky star way
to where he is splendid and generous
and where together we are a pear tree
   laden with light.

Reality

Shaking the seeds we unite
what is already
                    together.

"just open and open"
Goodnight, good night

oh dream!
oh what is!

in and out of the rose. . . . .
that I might be this tender

Yellow World Medicine

on the Yellow Road
        find medicine and rest.   Learn
about yourself.   Sit comfortably
amidst tansy, golden rod, dandelion, sunflowers,
        woodviolets.   Fill
pillows with the ripe, freely-given
splurge of cattails.

in Yellow splendor
        marry the Emperor's son
and bind like cords
        of golden-berried bittersweet

about the Treasure between you.

on closing the doors to winter,
1/10/88

you will never be alive again
and today the cold can rest, too.

It is no longer what I want
to remind
of what is not.

Your great long body
no more entails mine

and there's no one now
to hold the cold
space where you were.

Amnesia, no loss

           Really, what is there to know
about   myself?   Likewise
           there seems no knowing.

Forsythia Branches in a Vase
During February Sesshin

On the first day of retreat
I cut and brought them inside.
For three weeks now
I have sat almost
every moment
beside them
as the flowers have opened
and yet I've never seen
them actually make a move.

Only noticed
first the buds had flexed
apart from the branch,
then a bit of yellow had unfurled
more and more.

Burst!   one would say
who had just walked
into the room; one who had not
been sitting here patiently

waiting to see the plant act.
Anyone else but me
would see
the quality of suddenness
right within the definity
of yellow petals.

Perhaps their very stillness
is their opening force
which does not exist
as motion as such
on this plane
and is, apart from stillness,
invisible to me.

Or perhaps Forsythia is shy,
not public in advance
only in display,
and simply waited
til I turned my head away
to flower
bit by bit
as these branches have
that are now
fully in bloom.

Let the Forsythia flower
its unnoticeable way!
There's no defining it!
I must be the one
to change!
I shall pretend
to have entered
just now
this room
where the yellow flower blooms.

2/16/88

like coming to the surface
from a long, deep dive:
breath at last!
I am!

memory

memory
is just my mind.
what happened
has gone by.

do it in splendor
like every other cosmic thing
does it

they ask for so little.
As long as I give them water
my beautiful cyclamen are poised
for weeks
in their own perfection.

even in noise,
        the silence.
even in stillness,
        the song.

                    listening,
        I hear your great peace,
        a river
        deep underground.

        Running beneath the mountain
        of yourself
        peace thunders
        up and through.

        I know this river
        and also that
        loving you
        is my being.

        Cats are purring.
        I can find
        nothing
        to heal.

                    3/88

(poetry)

one's whole self cast out
like a net
to haul in
lord knows what

Your Wordlessly Perfect Body

how does it feel in your body
when you are centered and whole?

How does the sunflower feel?
How does Brace Cove feel
in the sunlight
      in the moonlight
in the wake of the wordlessly perfect
conjunctions of the moon and Venus?

When you don't have to think
or reason your way to compensation
as if your fear did not exist: how
does that feel?

Maybe there is wholeness already: well
being is already oneself, God, "of the same";
and a *simple* matter
without debt, desert or apart.

I find some mere joke inhibits this.

Whose poke it is

      really doesn't matter.

For the jokester vanishes

      in our delight and thankfulness.

                        5/2/88

White Mountain

how *would* I have known

you were my body

until I could be

my body my self?

one of those great surprises!

All of these years — 23 —

I've come here — not even

to that many other mountains — up high

"away from" complexities

            and obsessions.

I used to feel

when it was time to go back

that I was having to leave behind

what meant the most to me:

what I felt of "spirit,"

myself at best and beauty,

your openness, the softness,

intensity and utter exposure
of alpine plants, the hawks and crows

whose silhouettes in flight against the valley
and further slopes
are lavish in outline; the fresh, gay,
grassy, croppy hilltops that are just
like being in love
and irrevocably vulnerable simplicity.

All of this seemed "different"
from me and accessible — remotely
at that — only by being on the mountain.

In the first years
while climbing
my leg would drag
and I had no breath.   My body
had such pain but my spirit
— as I distinguished — soared
and spread and I longed
for more, for pervasion, for disappearance

into the being of the mountain.
I wanted to lose myself
and come out on the other side
of pain.

                 Through the years of healing
it's this body, really, you have kept for me.
Stored away and taken out, like for best,
on the days when I would walk strengthening
on the sky-touching paths marked by quartz shakes
from the dragon's sparkling
tail   and I would bathe
in the streams I could not cross
clothed.   Those times I tried on
this body you had held safe

until I learned
the really not-so-hidden and delicious
secrets of physics
from which I am
now not apart   from which spirit
is not held separate.

Now I am a mountain also!
I am myself.   Finally you have given
me my body.   Friends and tourists
complain of the wind
at my summit

and nestle out of the weather
in my spruce arms
and groves.

Thanks to you I am free, a physical being
in the physical world.
So what does this mean
to you, Body Keeper Mtn?
With all the energy you must have now,
unconcerned about me,
you are free to be........ what ?
Undivided Being Mtn, my lifetime
would know you
as you are.

— for Christopher

"(The) signs of Wilderness are everywhere"

        you said.   Most vividly,

as I see it, in *your* heart

the wild apples May-flower, the migrant

warblers with no conscience of audience

pelt the sky and all around

with their songs as if

there were no tomorrow.   Weedy

golden moments

self-seed the acreage.

but I know what you mean:

as we drive past the no nonsense housing

along Rte 133

coming home to Gloucester

      from Paradise.

There's really nothing to stop It

from breaking through the roadway

[37]

at any moment

or property lines, safety restrictions,

city planning, rural planning, war

zones, gates, plazas, yard sales, run-

ways, shoe stores, railroads, sanitary

landfills ——

the thickest

hardest, densest, abuse, torture,

hatred, ignorance, suffering

is no front for the fearless

bittersweet or burdock. dandelions, wild apples,

blackberries. . . . . .

At any moment

the insistences of civilization

could give way

to themselves.   Of that

we see signs

as we pass by.

6/88

Even there are cracks in our minds

for the green things to poke through.

Or maybe thanks to their poking

the cracks are there

and plant action furthers

plant action until the burdock,

elder, dandelion, golden rod, plaintain,

mullein, clover, St. Johnswort, knotweed,

soapwort, roses, locust, willow

and maple

just break up

the whole damn layer

of asphalt

        of mind

and we are at play

                in the fields again.

           6/88

It's death to smell a rose!

Inhale the fragrance

of a wild seaside rose

and who are you?   what's

left of identity

to recall

one's complaints

or comparisons or even praises?

On earth

the dare is out:

      smell the roses!

      walk in the gloaming!

      love your lover

          and be loved!

6/88

How wild is wild?
How wild will I get to be?
Is there a place

    I will pass beyond

or a moment of time

    and then. . . . .

or demarcation of some other

    coordinate or hearthline

of the way

I now know myself

beyond which. . . . . . . .wilderness begins?

I think it will all happen here.

I think the very stones and beaches

marsh coves, hills and fields

branches of bayberry, red cedar

    and shad

cranesbill, violets, moss

    and kelp

and their frequenting creatures

that I love and know

      as wild

will be even more so

and I among them.

2/89

The Crane Dance

(Relaxing in a Brutal World)

because the cranes are dancing.

because this space shines with their dancing

our minds can change

      be unconfined

and be aware of our reality

      of rhythm and connection.

In the Crane Dance

there is no unrelated aspect of being.

So we find violence

      is now unactable; no "other"

upon whom to act.

In the space made by the cranes' shine

there's no way to initiate deceit.

There are no weapons

no rape

no torment of animals

no ownership of land

no —

no longer in our minds

is there a means to conceive

      of doing harm.   There are no more

wounds.

because we are dancing

we are cranes

and make this space alive.

We dance the shining mind change,

      boundless connections that are we.

In the shining crane dance space

our bodies are aware

that we cannot be hurt; it is no longer

in our nature to be hurt; and our nature

now expresses

      this inviolability.

The Crane Dance is knowing this:

that to be a woman means no harm anywhere

possibly can be done and what's more now

      we can open and open

      endlessly to permit

this changing space of minds

        as the cranes dance.

LINDA CRANE (1945-2000) was a poet, naturalist, shamanic practitioner, and Zen Buddhist. She was born in Winchester, grew up in Duxbury, and spent most of her adult life in Gloucester, Massachusetts. Her literary associates included Robert Kelly, Charles Stein, Charles Olson, and Gerrit Lansing. She published two books of poetry (as Linda Parker) during her lifetime: *Graphite* (Tansy Press 1980) and *Seabirds* (Fathom Press 1980). She shared her work generously, often typing up fresh copies of poems to give to friends, and was well known throughout the Cape Ann area for both her poetry readings and her shamanic practice. In the late 1990s she wrote and gave public performances of two operas: *Spring* and *Anacaona*, singing her own compositions. She left a group of manuscripts prepared for publication at her death. *How Wild?*, subtitled in manuscript *She Speaks for Herself*, is the first of these to be published by her estate.